AFRICA

MW00883491

FROG

All-in-one guide book on African

dwarf frog care and keeping for

basic beginners

CHARLES CHAVEZ

TABLE OF CONTENTS

CHAPTER ONE

INTRODUCTION

The African dwarf frog (Hymenochirus sp.) is a sub-Saharan African aquatic amphibian. Because of their small size, ease of maintenance, and distinctive characteristics, these little frogs are popular pets. They are most commonly found in slow-moving freshwater streams, ponds, and swamps, and they have adapted to surviving in both stagnant and flowing water. African dwarf frogs are totally aquatic and spend their whole lives in water, only coming to the surface to breathe air. They are well-known for their active and inquisitive attitude, and can be seen swimming, investigating their surroundings, and even vocalizing.

HISTORY

The African dwarf frog has a lengthy and fascinating history that dates back thousands of years. The ancient Egyptians were the first to record these tiny amphibians, which they kept as pets in decorative pools. They were also highly esteemed by the ancient Greeks, who believed that frogs possessed medicinal characteristics and could treat a variety of illnesses.

African dwarf frogs have long been praised for their beauty, charm, and unusual mannerisms. They gained popularity among European naturalists in the 1800s, who were drawn to their watery lifestyle and odd anatomy. Scientists began to investigate the frogs in greater depth, and they quickly became a focus of considerable curiosity and inquiry.

African dwarf frogs were first imported into the United States as pets in the early 1900s, and they immediately acquired appeal as an easy-to-care-for and fascinating pet. African dwarf frogs are still a popular choice for new and seasoned pet owners alike, and can be found in pet stores and aquariums all over the world.

Despite their popularity, African dwarf frogs are threatened in the wild by a variety of factors, including habitat degradation and pollution. As a result, several conservation initiatives are being undertaken to safeguard these intriguing amphibians and their habitats for future generations to enjoy.

PHYSICAL CHARACTERISTICS

The African dwarf frog is a small aquatic amphibian with a peculiar look that distinguishes it from other kinds of frogs. They grow to be about 1.5-2 inches long, with a round, plump body and short legs. Their skin is smooth and moist, and the hue ranges from brown to olive to green to gray, with black dots or stripes.

The African dwarf frog's webbed feet are one of its most distinguishing physical characteristics, as they are perfectly designed for swimming and allow the frog to travel gracefully through the water. Their toes also include small suction cups, allowing them to adhere to rocks and other objects.

African dwarf frogs have flattened heads, big eyes, and a toothless mouth. They have two nostrils for breathing air at the water's surface. They also have a distinct lateral line system that allows them to feel vibrations in the water and navigate their surroundings.

Male African dwarf frogs are slightly smaller than females and have little, dark nuptial pads on their forearms that they utilize to hold females during mating. Overall, the morphological traits of the African dwarf frog are ideal for their aquatic existence, making them an interesting and one-of-a-kind companion.

LIFESPAN

African dwarf frogs' lifespans can vary widely based on a variety of factors such as diet, environment, and heredity. These frogs can survive in captivity for an average of 5-7 years, while some have been known to live for up to 10 years or more.

Proper care and a nutritious meal are crucial for the survival of African dwarf frogs. These frogs demand a clean and well-kept aquatic environment with adequate water quality, temperature, and illumination. They also require a varied and nutritious diet that includes both live and cooked meals in order to obtain all of the important elements they require to stay healthy.

Overcrowding, poor water quality, and an unsuitable diet can dramatically limit the lifespan of African dwarf frogs, therefore it is critical to give them with the finest care possible to help them thrive.

CHAPTER TWO

BEHAVIOR OF AFRICAN DWARF FROG

African dwarf frogs are a common choice for pet owners due to their fascinating and amusing nature. These aquatic frogs have a curious and sociable temperament, and they are quite playful and active.

Fully aquatic, African dwarf frogs spend the most of their time swimming and scouting out their surroundings. They are adept swimmers who glide through the water with grace thanks to their webbed feet and strong legs. They are also quite flexible and can survive in both still and moving water, but they choose the former.

The vocalization of African dwarf frogs is among their most fascinating habits. These frogs produce a variety of noises for social interaction and communication, such as chirping, trilling, and croaking. They are also renowned for being highly tactile beings, frequently interacting with one another by touching one another with their webbed feet.

Since they are gregarious creatures, African dwarf frogs are frequently housed in groups in aquariums. While they should be kept with species that are comparable in size and temperament, they are often calm and get along with other aquatic species, such as fish and snails.

HABITAT

Native to sub-Saharan Africa, the African dwarf frog can be found there in a variety of freshwater habitats such as streams, ponds, swamps, and marshes. As long as the water quality is excellent and there is enough cover and hiding places, these frogs are highly versatile and can thrive in both stagnant and flowing water.

African dwarf frogs are found in close proximity to other aquatic species including fish, snails, and insects, which they eat, in their natural habitat. Being mainly nocturnal, they spend the day lurking behind rocks, plants, and other debris during the night actively searching for food.

African dwarf frogs need an aquarium that closely resembles their native habitat, is well-kept, and the right size to keep them in captivity. They require filtered, clear water that is the right temperature and illumination, as well as lots of cover like rocks, plants, and caverns.

While larger aquariums are advised for keeping numerous frogs or other aquatic species, at least 10 gallons is the best aquarium size for African dwarf frogs. To guarantee they receive a varied diet that is both balanced and nutrient-dense, it is essential to offer both live and prepared foods.

SETTING UP A TANK

To preserve the health and well-being of these unusual aquatic amphibians, setting up a tank for African dwarf frogs involves considerable study and planning. The following are some measures to take while setting up a tank for African dwarf frogs:

1. Select the appropriate aquarium size: A tank of at least 10 gallons is recommended for African dwarf frogs, however larger aquariums are advised for raising numerous frogs or other aquatic species. Make sure the tank has a sturdy lid to keep other animals out and prevent escape.

2. Add substrate: To protect their sensitive skin, African dwarf frogs require a soft substrate, such as sand or fine gravel. Sharp or abrasive substrates should be avoided since they might cause skin irritation or harm.

3. Provide hiding places: Because African dwarf frogs are nocturnal, they require a lot of hiding places, such as rocks, bushes, and caves.

Make careful to provide a variety of hiding spots within the tank.

4. Install a filter: A filter is required to keep the tank's water clean and healthy. Select a filter that is suitable for the size of your tank and is intended for use in aquatic conditions.

5. Maintain adequate water quality: To survive, African dwarf frogs require clean, well-maintained water. To keep the water clean and healthy, monitor the water quality on a regular basis and execute regular water changes.

6. Provide adequate lighting: To preserve their natural circadian cycles, African dwarf frogs require a consistent light cycle. To provide adequate lighting conditions for your frogs, use a full-spectrum aquarium lamp.

7. Provide a variety diet: African dwarf frogs require a varied diet that includes both live and prepared meals. Provide a variety of diets, such as bloodworms, brine shrimp, and commercial frog pellets, to ensure they get all the necessary nutrients.

CHAPTER THREE

CARE REQUIREMENT

Although the care requirements for African dwarf frogs are very straightforward, it is important to meet their unique requirements in order to maintain their health and welfare. The following are important considerations for taking care of African dwarf frogs:

1. Tank size: African dwarf frogs need tanks that are at least 10 gallons in volume and at least 12 inches deep. A bigger tank can be useful because it gives the frogs more room to swim and explore.

2. Water quality: Clean, well-oxygenated water is necessary for African dwarf frogs. The pH level should be between 6.5 and 7.5, and the water temperature should be kept between 72 and 82°F (22 and 28°C). To maintain the best possible water quality, it is crucial to undertake routine water changes.

3. Filtration: To keep water pure, a good filtration system is necessary. The filter needs to be the right size for the tank and able to deliver enough water flow and oxygenation.

4. Substrate: Fine sand or small pebbles is suggested as a substrate since it offers the frogs a natural environment in which to burrow and explore.

5. Illumination: Although ambient illumination can be advantageous for African dwarf frogs' health and well-being, special lighting is not necessary for them.

6. Nutrition: As carnivores, African dwarf frogs need a diversified diet of meaty items such brine shrimp, brine worms, and tiny pieces of fish or shrimp. It's crucial to give them just enough to fill them up for a few minutes once or twice a day.

7. Handling: African dwarf frogs are delicate creatures and should be handled with care. It is preferable to stay away from them until absolutely essential because stress might be bad for their health.

8. Monitoring: To make sure African dwarf frogs are strong and thriving, regular observation and monitoring are necessary. Look out for signs of illness or injury, such as abnormal behavior, changes in appetite, or physical abnormalities.

African dwarf frogs can live long, happy lives and add joy and curiosity to your home aquarium by receiving the proper care.

FEEDING AND NUTRITION

African dwarf frogs are carnivorous amphibians that consume a range of small aquatic creatures like insects, crabs, and snails in the wild. In order to meet their nutritional demands while in captivity, a balanced and wholesome food is important.

The following are some recommendations for feeding and nourishing African dwarf frogs:

1. Provide a variety of foods: African dwarf frogs need both live and prepared items in their diets. Offer a variety of foods to make sure they get all the nutrients they require to keep healthy, such as bloodworms, brine shrimp, and commercial frog pellets.

2. Refrain from overeating: Overeating can result in health issues like obesity, digestive disorders, and water quality issues. Only give your frogs as much food as they can finish in a few minutes, and take out any leftovers from the tank.

3. Feed in the evening: Because African dwarf frogs are nocturnal and more active in the evening, it is better to feed them after the lights have been turned out. They will have plenty of time to find and eat their food as a result.

4. Take vitamin supplements: African dwarf frogs may need extra vitamins and minerals to stay healthy. You can add commercial vitamin and mineral supplements made for amphibians to their diet.

5. Provide live food: Bloodworms and brine shrimp are two examples of live prey that African dwarf frogs enjoy pursuing and catching. Their natural eating behavior can be stimulated by providing live food.

HANDLING AND CARE

Handling African dwarf frogs should be avoided to the greatest extent possible. These frogs have sensitive skin that is readily damaged, and if handled excessively, they may grow stressed. However, handling may be required at times, such as during tank maintenance or veterinarian care. Here are some guidelines for dealing with African dwarf frogs:

1. **Wet your hands:** Wet your hands with aquarium water before touching an African dwarf frog. This will help to keep their sensitive skin safe.

2. **Support their body:** When taking up an African dwarf frog, use both hands to support its body

and avoid crushing them forcefully. Their skin is permeable, and any abrasive pressure can cause them harm.

3. Avoid abrupt movements: When handling African dwarf frogs, move slowly and carefully, as abrupt movements might surprise and stress them.

4. Return them to the water as soon as possible: African dwarf frogs can hold their breath for several minutes, but it is critical to return them to the water as soon as possible after handling to avoid stress or oxygen shortage.

Aside from handling, here are some other guidelines for caring for African dwarf frogs:

1. Provide a proper habitat: African dwarf frogs require a clean, appropriately sized tank that resembles their natural environment. They require clean and filtered water, as well as adequate water temperature and lighting conditions, as well as a plentiful supply of hiding places such as rocks, plants, and caves.

2. Examine water quality: It is critical to periodically examine water quality to ensure the health and well-being of your frogs. Water factors such as pH, ammonia, and nitrite levels should be tested on a regular basis.

3. Provide a broad and balanced diet that includes both live and prepared meals, and prevent overfeeding.

4. Maintain proper hygiene: carefully wash your hands before and after handling the aquarium or any equipment, and avoid touching your face or mouth when caring for the frogs.

5. Avoid stressful situations: African dwarf frogs are sensitive to environmental changes and might become upset if disturbed or exposed to loud noises or bright lights. Avoid abrupt changes in water temperature or other environmental conditions, and keep your frogs in a calm and tranquil setting.

CHAPTER FOUR

BREEDING AND REPRODUCTION

The breeding habits and reproductive methods of African dwarf frogs are well recognized. Here's a detailed look at African dwarf frog breeding and reproduction:

Breeding:

1. Choose breeding pairs: For breeding, select African dwarf frogs that are healthy, mature, and sexually mature. African dwarf frogs' sex can be determined by the size and form of their body. Males are often shorter and leaner than females. Females have a broader, rounder figure, and a bulging abdomen if they are pregnant (carrying eggs).

2. Provide a proper breeding environment: Provide a separate breeding tank for the frogs with sufficient lighting and water conditions. The breeding tank should be larger than the usual tank and provide numerous hiding spots, like as plants or rocks. It is also critical to keep the frogs' water temperature and pH levels at appropriate ranges.

3. Condition the frogs: Provide a balanced diet of live and prepared items to prepare the frogs for breeding. You may also replicate the seasonal changes that occur in their native habitat by progressively lowering the water temperature. This chilling time may aid in the initiation of reproductive activities in frogs.

4. Study breeding behavior: When male African dwarf frogs are ready to mate, they make a "whine" or croaking sound. They may also engage in courtship behavior, such as pursuing or clasping onto the female's back. They will discharge their eggs and sperm into the water after the male has grasped onto the female. The eggs will sink to the tank's bottom and stick to plants or other surfaces.

Reproduction

Within 24-48 hours of mating, the eggs develop into tadpoles. Tadpoles will feed on their yolk sacs at first, then on minute food particles. To prevent the growth of hazardous germs, remove any unfertilized eggs or dead tadpoles from the tank. Tadpoles will go through a number of modifications over the course of several weeks before becoming adult frogs. You will need to offer proper food and water conditions for the tadpoles to thrive during this time. When the tadpoles have matured, you can place them in the main tank alongside adult African dwarf frogs. It is critical that the tank has enough of hiding spots and enough space for all of the frogs to coexist together.

COMMON HEALTH ISSUES AND PREVENTIVE CARE

African dwarf frogs are generally healthy and resilient species when kept under perfect conditions, however they are prone to various health problems. Below are some of the most common health issues that African dwarf frogs may encounter, as well as suggestions for how to avoid them:

1. Bacterial infections

African dwarf frogs are vulnerable to bacterial infections, which can cause skin redness or inflammation, hazy eyes, or lethargy. Bacterial infections are frequently induced by contaminated water, overcrowding, or other stressors. Preventing bacterial infections, maintaining ideal water conditions, avoiding overcrowding, and providing proper nutrition are all priorities.

2. Fungal infections

Fungal infections in African dwarf frogs can emerge as white, fluffy growths on the skin or fins. Fungal infections are frequently caused by poor water quality or stress, and they can be avoided by maintaining ideal water conditions and giving adequate nourishment.

3. Parasites

African dwarf frogs are vulnerable to parasites such as flukes and anchor worms, which can cause irritation, inflammation, and other symptoms. To avoid parasites, keep appropriate water conditions, quarantine fresh frogs before bringing them to the tank, and avoid adding unknown plants or animals.

4. Nutritional deficits

African dwarf frogs require a varied and balanced diet to stay healthy, and deficiencies in particular nutrients can cause health issues. A shortage of vitamin A, for example, might cause vision difficulties, but a lack of calcium can cause bone problems. Provide a varied and balanced diet of meaty meals such as brine shrimp, bloodworms, and other aquatic invertebrates to avoid nutritional deficits.

5. Stress

African dwarf frogs are sensitive creatures that can get stressed as a result of a variety of causes such as poor water quality, overcrowding, or insufficient hiding places. Maintain appropriate water conditions, limit overpopulation, provide plenty of hiding places, and handle the frogs gently to reduce stress.

CONCLUSION

The African dwarf frog is a little aquatic species with a distinct look and fascinating activities. They are low-maintenance and can be a beautiful and entertaining addition to a home aquarium. Proper care, such as optimal water conditions, filtration, and a well-balanced diet, can help keep them healthy and thriving. Despite their toughness, they are susceptible to some health conditions, thus they must be monitored and observed on a regular basis. Overall, the African dwarf frog is a wonderful and fascinating species that may please its owners while also serving as a fascinating subject for observation and study.

THANKS FOR READING

Made in United States
Orlando, FL
15 August 2024

50387377R00030